D1505559

The Nannini Guide

Navigating Your Way to Successful Transfer to the University of California

First Edition

Daniel L. Nannini, M.S.

DLN
PUBLISHING

LIBRARY OF CONGRESS CATALOGING-IN-PUBLICATION DATA

Nannini, Dan.
   The Nannini Guide : navigating your way to successful
   transfer to the University of California / by Dan Nannini. --
   1st ed.
      p. cm.
   Includes bibliographical references.

   1. Students, Transfer of--California--Handbooks, manuals,
   etc. 2. University of California (System)--Entrance
   requirements. I. Title.

LB2360.N36 2002   378.1'09794
                                                   QB102-200287

Library of Congress Control Number: 2002091152

DLN Publishing, LLC
Culver City, CA 90230

Cover and interior design: Marilyn Hager
Author photo: Maria Bonin
Printed in the United States of America by Central Plains

1 2 5 7 9 8 6 4 2

*I dedicate this book to all those people in our lives
that inspire us to reach slightly farther than we think
we can realize; in my life, Mom and Dad were the first.*

Table of Contents

Acknowledgments: vi

Introduction: The Ten Commandments of Transfer vii

Chapter One: Attending A California Community College 1
Best Strategy for Transfer, Transferring from Other Schools

Chapter Two: Defining the University of California 5
Minimum University Admission Requirements, Campus Organization

Chapter Three: Completing Sixty UC Transferable Semester Units . 9
Transferring with Mixed Records, Minimum and Maximum Units, Units from Colleges and Universities, Unit Limitations

Chapter Four: GPA and Lower Division Major Requirements . . 19
Impacted and Competitive Majors, Enhancing Admissibility

Chapter Five: General Education 49
Choices for GE, IGETC, IGETC after Transfer

Chapter Six: How About Getting Admitted with An Easier Major, Then Switching When I Get There? 55
Backdoor Strategy Pros and Cons, Major Change Policies

Chapter Seven: Applying, Appealing, and Guaranteed Admission Programs 65
Deadlines, Non-Fall Admission Opportunities, Writing Personal Statement

VERY IMPORTANT NOTE AND CONCLUSION 77

Glossary: 79

Appendix A: 85

Appendix B: 87

Acknowledgements

My deep gratitude to Brenda Johnson-Benson, my Dean and former Santa Monica College Transfer Center Director, who has been the best boss and friend one could hope to have and has set a high standard of excellence for delivering transfer information. The entire SMC Counseling Faculty's dedication and professionalism has motivated me to do my best, and keeps me on my toes with their insightful questions to better help students reach their goals. And last, but most certainly not least, my sincere respect to the men and women in the Outreach and Admission offices throughout the University of California who, patiently and tirelessly, share their time and energy with students and community college faculty well beyond the call of duty. Also, my thanks to Estela Narrie and Judith DeLorca for editorial assistance.

Introduction

When I was a counselor at UCLA, I would get new transfer students in my office that would ask me how long it would take them to graduate from UCLA. More often than not I would tell them it would take longer than two years to complete their requirements to graduate. Their first reaction was usually confusion. They thought that, having just finished two years of college, they had only two more years to go. Then, I would explain to them that they had indeed completed two years of college and met minimum entrance requirements, but they had not completed the appropriate sequence of courses, for either general education requirements or major requirements, to truly qualify as juniors. I would then point out a particular class or classes that they took that didn't help them complete either a general education or major requirement. Now, their confusion would turn to anger, "My counselor told me this class would transfer!" I would tell them, yes, it did transfer, but the question never asked, and subsequently never answered, was **"Does this class satisfy either a general education or major requirement for me, and if not, do I need this elective?"**

This Guide is my attempt to answer that question and save the transfer student from disappointment and wasted time.

When I left UCLA and started counseling at Santa Monica College (a California community college), I was determined not be one of those less-than-accurate community college counselors. I was going to set an example of timely, accurate, and precise information. Then, I made a very important and humbling discovery. The UCs were not always timely, accurate, and/or precise in providing information to the community college counselors.

Thirteen years have passed since I left UCLA. The communication is better between the UCs and community colleges, and the information has become voluminous. This Guide attempts to organize and impart this information to students, parents, and professionals, with a minimum amount of jargon and emphasis on two primary goals:

- To make a student attractive for admission as a transfer student.
- To help a student graduate in a timely manner after admission.

A student once asked me at the end of counseling session, "Are there any questions that I didn't ask?" This Guide contains those questions and answers.

This guide does not explore which campus or major "fits" a student best. I recommend consulting the UC publication *Introducing the University of California*, conferring with counselors and UC Outreach personnel. Talk to alumni and current students, and when possible, visit the campus. This guide does provide critical information to enhance admissibility!

There are ten essential strategies that the serious transfer student must memorize. Let's name them *The Ten Commandments of Transfer* for easy reference:

THE 10 COMMANDMENTS OF TRANSFER

1. Complete the most possible lower division requirements in your major <u>prior</u> to applying. (The more the better!)

2. Complete 60 transferable semester units (or 90 transferrable quarter units) at least two terms prior to the time you arrive at the UC campus of your choice.

3. Earn the highest GPA possible in your lower division major requirements.

4. Earn the highest overall GPA possible in all UC transferrable courses.

5. Complete the required UC transferable math and English courses prior to applying.

6. Attend a California Community College.

7. Apply on time.

8. Complete the I.G.E.T.C. or campus specific general education requirements prior to enrolling at the UC you have been admitted to.

9. Write a great personal essay when you submit your application.

10. Complete the UC minimum admission requirements for transfer applicants.

Ideally, this list is to be absorbed in its entirety, not attended to "sort of" or half-heartedly. If a student "sort of" attends to these suggestions, their application could be attended to "sort of". The student might even be automatically denied. By following this list in its entirety, the student maximizes their chances for admission, merit scholarships and graduating two years after they arrive on the campus of their choice.

These suggestions to maximize admission consideration are not all set in stone; this Guide will try to help the student determine the flexibility they have to enter one of the UC campuses.

There are two critical factors for the student to ponder while preparing to transfer. First, while in college, the stiffest competition they face is themselves. Anything less than their full effort and achievement will make reaching their goal more difficult. Ultimately, the transfer student is compared to other applicants who are striving toward the same thing: admission.

Second, a student must apply and have the university determine admissibility. This book is a guide; the University of California publications are a guide, and what counselors, teachers, outreach counselors, and friends say is a guide. Ultimately, it is the student's responsibility to stay aware of changing requirements, slap down the money, fill out the application, and mail it, otherwise, they will never know. If a student doesn't apply, they won't get in.

One of my favorite students came to Santa Monica College right out of high school, and did very poor work. He dropped out, got a job at the Post Office, and worked for a few years. He came back to SMC and started cleaning up his transcripts by repeating D's and F's. During this process, he applied to UCLA four times, and got rejected each time. On the fifth try, he said he couldn't bear to wait for the decision, and could I find out for him. So, I called some friends in low places and was told he was admitted. I called him at the Post Office and relayed the good news. He said he was jubilant, he just wanted to scream and dance for joy, but because of where he worked, his actions might be misinterpreted.

It is that victory of results and the pleasure of that individual's future possibilities that helped inspire this guide.

Chapter
One

Attending A California
Community College

Attending a California Community College (CCC) will increase the chances for getting the thick, 9 x 12 envelope (which means the student is "in") instead of the thin, legal-sized envelope (which means the student is not.) Why? Let me show you the numbers:

Percentage of Fall 2001 Transfer Students admitted to the UCs from California Community Colleges of All Transfers Admitted*	
Berkeley	79%
Davis	84%
Irvine	82%
Los Angeles	85%
Riverside	87%
San Diego	88%
Santa Barbara	85%
Santa Cruz	82%

*From a publication of the University of California for the 2001 Counselor Conferences

There is a story that gets passed around counselor conferences about the transfer student from Harvard with a 3.1 GPA that couldn't get into any of the 5 most competitive UCs because he was not transferring from a California Community College. Community College students need a place to transfer in order to finish a baccalaureate degree, whereas, university students can complete their degree at the university. Also, it is important to note, the UCs accept a high percentage of CCC students because "The undergraduate admission policy of the University of California is guided by the University's commitment to serve the people of California and needs of the state, within the framework of the California Master Plan for Higher Education." (Answers for Transfers, 2002–03)

Is it possible to transfer from an institution other than a California Community College? Yes, but realize that the next tier of students accepted as transfers are inter-campus transfers. Inter-campus transfers are students at one UC campus that want to go to another UC campus.

If a student didn't attend a CCC or another UC, then, they are in the third tier of transfer applicants, which seriously diminishes the chances of admission. But remember, if the student doesn't apply, they'll never know.

When the UC started giving priority to California Community College transfers, I was seeing students enrolling at Santa Monica College (SMC) the last term prior to transfer from their four-year universities. Aware of this tactic, the individual UC campuses, a few years ago, began "tightening the reins", and each came up with specific definitions of a California Community College transfer student. Now, happily, there is one definition of what constitutes a CCC transfer. That definition is as follows:

- Complete 30 transferable semester units at a California Community College
- Complete at least two regular terms at a California Community College (not Summer session or Intersession)
- Last school attended must be a California Community College

The next question a student might ask is "How do I choose which community college to attend?" The student needs to choose a community college based on their needs and desires. Some students choose based on location, a great job or family obligations require them to make this a priority. Other students want to attend college away from home, so they choose a community college near the institution to which they want to transfer. Some may call that transfer institution to inquire, "Tell me the top five community colleges that send you the most students." There are rumors that if you attend a specific community college, you will increase your chance for admission at particular UCs. This is not entirely true. Certain community colleges do have specific honors programs that might give you an advantage for admission to specific UCs in particular majors, but these programs are not comprehensive. I had a student who drove 60 miles one-way in LA traffic to attend Santa Monica College because he had heard we offered a guaranteed admission program with UCLA. Our Scholar's Program offers "priority consideration" for students that want entry into the College of Letters and Science at UCLA. My student wanted to enroll in the School of Engineering! The moral of the story is, make sure to ask detailed questions of the institution before attending. Chapter 7 discusses which California community colleges have specific programs to enhance chances for admission to the UC of choice.

Defining the University of California

The University of California system has nine campuses (actually ten, but UC Merced isn't accepting students until 2004), eight of which grant Bachelor's degrees (Bachelor of Arts, Bachelor of Science, Bachelor of Fine Arts, Bachelor of Science in Nursing). The locations of the eight campuses are Berkeley, Davis, Irvine Los Angeles, Riverside, San Diego, Santa Barbara, and Santa Cruz. The ninth campus is in San Francisco and offers only graduate degrees and professional schools.

Each campus has a variety of separate schools or colleges. Within these schools and colleges, there are specific majors. To graduate with one of these majors, you must complete University requirements, college or school requirements, and major requirements. To get successfully admitted as a transfer student, you **must** determine the specific transfer admission requirements related to the university, school or college, and major. This chapter will address university admission requirements and Chapters 3, 4, and 5 will address admission and graduation requirements of the various schools or colleges and majors.

Minimum University Admission Requirements for Transfers

There are three ways to satisfy the University of California minimum transfer admission requirements. Two of the three ways are related to how well you did in high school, the specific course work you completed, and your performance on standardized tests (like SAT or ACT). If you want to transfer with less than 60 transferable semester units, you must use one of these two methods for transfer admission. Since 99% of transfer applicants I see don't use the requirements based on high school performance, I refer those that think they might be eligible from high school to Appendix "A" in the back of this book or one of four UC publications titled:

Quick Reference for Counselors
Introducing the University
Answers for Transfers
The Undergraduate Application to the University of California

These publications are located on the Web at:
www.ucop.edu/pathways

The most common way to satisfy minimum University of California transfer admission requirements is to:

Complete 60 UC transferable semester or 90 quarter units of college work with a minimum 2.4 GPA (2.8 for non-residents.) Those units must contain the following specific coursework:

- Two English composition courses (remember, they must be UC transferable, at least 3 semester or 4 quarter units, and a minimum "C" grade in each).

- One Math course (remember, it must be UC transferable, 3 semester or 4 quarter units, with a minimum "C" grade). [**Note**: All transferable math courses have intermediate algebra or higher as a pre-requisite.]

- Four courses chosen from 2 or more of the following subject areas:

- Arts & Humanities
- Social & Behavioral Science
- Physical & Biological Science

(Remember, the courses must be UC transferable, a minimum of 3 semester or 4 quarter units, and they must be completed with a "C" or better.)

Now, keep in mind, the requirements that I just discussed are the <u>minimum needed to have your application considered</u>. In other words, you have qualified to compete, but it doesn't mean you've earned the gold medal.

Chapter
Three

Complete Sixty
UC Transferable
Semester Units

Units/Credits/Hours

So what is a "unit"? A unit is approximately 1 hour in class per week per semester. I have just described a semester unit. There are some schools that are on the quarter system, and they give quarter unit credit. In fact, all UC schools are on the quarter system, except Berkeley, which is on the semester system. One semester unit equals 1.5 quarter units, or 1 quarter unit equals .67 semester units. If a student is coming from a quarter system, the student must complete 90 UC transferable quarter units for admission (90 Quarter Units x 2/3 = 60 semester units).

The word "transferable" is very critical when discussing units. All California Community Colleges have Transferable Course Agreements (TCAs) with the University of California. There is someone in the Office of the President of the University of California whose job is to determine which California Community College courses are transferable. The general guideline to determine transferability is that the course must be taught for graduation credit somewhere in the UC system. If a student takes a course at a college not in the CCC, the individual UC campus will determine the transferability using general guidelines from the Office of the President of the University of California.

Transferable units can be earned by two methods. One way is to complete units at an accredited school, college, or university. Each UC campus and all CCC are accredited by the Western Association of Schools and Colleges (WASC). For the units to be transferable, they must be completed at an institution that is a member of the WASC, or at a school that has a reciprocity agreement with WASC. For example, the Northwest Association of Schools and Colleges is the accrediting body in that part of the United States, and there is an agreement that a course at their school will count for credit at a school that is a member of the Western Association of Schools and Colleges. **Beware**: most vocational, trade and technical schools are accredited by organizations that use different standards, and those schools don't have reciprocity agreements with WASC. I once had a student that came for help to fill out her application. When I looked at her transcripts, she had completed work from a vocational school in Canada, so I called UCLA and they told me "No way will those units transfer!" It delayed this woman's transfer by a year! She had no idea the units were not transferable. Always confirm course transferability with the campus the student is trying to enter.

The second way to earn credits is to have successfully completed the College Board Advanced Placement exams or the International Baccalaureate exams. A score of 3 or better on the AP exam or a score of 5 or higher on the IB exam will earn credit. **But a strong word of caution about these credits**. The University of California's publication, "A Quick Reference for Counselors," states:

"The credit may be Subject Credit, Graduation Credit, or credit toward General Education or Breadth

Requirements, *as determined by the evaluators at each campus.*" (The italics are mine.)

Each campus, and sometimes each school or college at that campus, interprets the results differently (sometimes, evaluators sitting right next to each other have different interpretations). I suggest calling the campus, school or college, and major department to determine the exact credit that will be awarded. When you get an answer, politely ask for the name and title of the person providing the information. Write this down, along with the date and time the information was received.

Be aware that even if a previous college gives specific course credit for one of these exams, the UC campuses use their own guidelines to award credit. For example, at Santa Monica College, a score of 3 or better on the Psychology AP is equivalent to our Introductory Psychology class. But, UCLA **does not** give specific credit for an Introductory Psychology course by passing the AP with a 3. Therefore, if this student wanted to be a Psychology major at UCLA (or any other major that required an Introductory Psychology course), they would be required to take SMC's Introductory Psychology course to satisfy the UCLA lower division major admission requirement. The AP exam would give units toward transfer, but only elective units. However, if the student passed the AP with a 4 or 5, they would receive course credit.

There are situations where a student can have too many units, especially if the student has attended more than one college or university in their academic career. The general rule is if a student has accumulated 80 or more transferable semester units, they will not be considered for admission. Each of the universities and colleges of the UC tweaks its interpretation of this rule a bit, and I will go into more detail later in this chapter.

If a student only attends a community college, the student can never have too many units. For any course completed after 70 units, a student will receive subject credit, but not unit credit. For example, a student takes Spanish 1 and when finished, the student has a grand total of 70 transferable semester units. However, the student needs Spanish 2 to satisfy a requirement. Completing Spanish 2 will result in recognition that the language requirement is completed without acknowledging any more units. Consequently, the student is given credit for the subject, but is not given any more units toward graduation. In my office, I keep a UCLA Degree Progress Report of a student that was admitted to UCLA with over 180 transferable semester units from two community colleges. I use this to show students that they can never take too many units at a community college.

There are some specific subjects that have unit limitations:

- Physical Education: Maximum of 4 semester units transfers.

- Pre-Calculus/Trigonometry: Maximum of 4 semester units transfers.

- Foreign Language: If a student attended a high school where the language of instruction was in a language other than English and takes that same foreign language that they were schooled in at the community college, they will not receive credit for it.

Unit Limitations and Admissions Danger for Students with Mixed Records

This section will discuss the danger of "mixed records" at each of the campuses, and specifically the schools and colleges at those campuses. A mixed record means the student has attended a university or baccalaureate granting college **and** a community college. The source of the following information was a handout distributed at the "Ensuring Transfer Success" conference.

Berkeley

The **College of Letters & Science** will not admit a student with more than 80 transferable semester units of credit from another university. If a student attends a university first and does not accrue 80 semester units and subsequently attends a CCC, the student can take as many units as they want at the CCC, and the total number of UC transferable units will not ever rise above 80. The student will receive subject credit for any courses taken after the 80 units.

The **College of Environmental Design** follows the Letters & Science rules, except its cut-off is 86 semester units.

The **Haas School of Business** combines the university and community college units regardless of which school is first attended. A student will not be considered for admission if the combined total is more than 80 units. If a student completes 10 semester units or less at a university, Haas will only count a maximum 70 semester units from a Community College, so it is impossible to exceed the 80 unit ceiling in that instance.

The **College of Chemistry** has a combined ceiling of 90 transferable semester units, of university and community college work, regardless which institution is first attended. If a student has 50 transferable semester units from a community college, the student can have 40 transferable semester units from a university. If the student has less than 20 transferable semester units from a university, then attended a community college, the student can never have too many units because the maximum allowed by the University from a CCC is 70 (70+20=90).

The **College of Engineering** works like the College of Chemistry, except its combined ceiling is 86 transferable semester units.

The **College of Natural Resources** has the same policy as the College of Chemistry.

Davis

The **College of Agriculture & Environmental Sciences, the College of Letters & Science**, and the **Division of Biological Sciences** review applications if the student has completed more than 80 transferable semester units, university and community college combined. Those with more than 80 semester units will only be admitted if, upon review and Dean's assessment, they can complete all their graduation requirements before the 225 quarter unit maximum. Units earned through College Board Advanced Placement (AP) Examinations or International Baccalaureate (IB) Higher Level Examinations are counted separately for this purpose. AP and IB units do not put applicants in jeopardy of being denied admission or of having an admissions decision delayed because of Dean's Review.

The College of Engineering does not discriminate based on units accrued. They admit the best candidates based on their review.

Irvine

Irvine does not have a limit on units completed at a four-year institution prior to enrolling at a community college. However, a minimum of the last 36 quarter units must be completed at UCI to earn a UCI degree.

Los Angeles

The **College of Letters and Science**: If a student attends a university first and completes 86 semester units or less, the student can subsequently take courses at the community college and not be in danger of taking too many units. Once a student completes a total of 70 UC transferable semester units (university and community college combined), they will receive only subject credit. Subject credit means the course will be acknowledged as completed and the subject mastered, but the actual unit value will not be added to the total.

If a student attends a community college first and then a university, the maximum number of units the student can complete at the university is the difference between the number of transferable community college units and 86.

Example: Student goes to SMC, completes 46 units, then transfers to Harvard. At Harvard, she decides she wants to go to UCLA. As long as the student does not complete more than 40 units she will still be considered for admission to the College of Letters & Science. (Her chances are almost zero however, because the last school she attended was not a community college. See Chapter 2.)

The **Schools and Colleges of Engineering, Arts & Architecture, and Theatre, Film, & Television** follow roughly the same guidelines but, on occasion, they will exceed the 86 semester unit maximum by a few units. This is reviewed on a case-by-case basis.

Riverside

All Riverside Schools and Colleges will review all applications of students which have four-year university attendance and a combined total of more than 101 transferable semester units. An applicant may be admitted upon review by the Dean if that student can complete a baccalaureate degree within the maximum limit of 216 quarter units.

San Diego

All UCSD schools and colleges will consider applications for admission if the student has completed 90 UC transferable semester units or less when combining previous university units with community college units.

However, there is a maximum of 70 UC transferable semester units allowed from a community college. Therefore, if a student attended a university first, and completed less than 20 UC transferable semester units, the student would never be in danger of completing more than 90 UC transferable semester units, because after completing 70 UC transferable semester units from a community college, the student will receive only subject credit.

Santa Barbara

UCSB does not accept applications from students who have earned 135 or more transferable quarter units (90 or more transferable semester units) from a combination of two year and four year institutions.

The **School of Engineering** will review applications of students with combined records of 90 transferable semester units or more, but acceptance is rare.

Santa Cruz

None of the schools or colleges will consider a student with combined records of university and community college units exceeding 90 transferable semester units (I am always suspicious when rules appear to be so rigid, but it sounds pretty definitive!)

	TRANSFERRING IN:		
	FALL	Winter	SPRING
Finish 60 transferable semester units by:	Spring prior to admission	Summer prior to admission	Fall prior to admission

Note: <u>Not</u> all campuses admit all terms. Please read chapter 7 on the application process.

Most schools want you to finish your 60 transferable semester units two terms prior to the term you set foot on the UC campus of your choice. (See diagram above)

For example, a student wants to enter Berkeley in the Fall of 2002. The student must complete 60 transferable semester units by the end of Spring 2002. Winter applicants are usually allowed to complete units in the Fall prior to admission, but if the 60 transferable semester units are completed in summer, the applicant is more attractive.

Are there exceptions? Sometimes, but only for very unusual circumstances that are beyond the control of the student. Unusual circumstances could be ill health or personal family emergencies. When, and if, those unusual circumstances arise, the student **must** immediately call the campus they are trying to enter and inform them of the dilemma.

If a student figures, "I'll finish this last class in the summer, what's the big deal?" believe me; Hell hath no fury like provisional admission requirements scorned! The offer of admission can be withdrawn. All schools admit more students than they need, assuming a certain percentage won't accept or will not meet the provisions of the provisional admission. If a student doesn't inform the UC campus what's going on, they are endangering their admission. UC admissions directors and their staff detest canceling offers of admission, so it is best to keep them informed when circumstances change.

Chapter
Four

GPA and Lower Division Major Requirements

Admission is based on a combination of factors depending on the individual applicant. No one gets into the UC based on any one factor. As stated in the Introduction, all "The 10 Commandments of Transfer" are important. Let's focus in this chapter on "Commandments" 1 and 3.

If a student has a 4.0 GPA, but no lower division coursework in the major completed and/or less than 60 UC transferable units, and was not eligible from high school, the student is most likely not getting in. If a student has all of the lower division major coursework done, 60 UC transferable units, math & English, and 2.3 GPA, they're not getting in. The variations are endless. **A student can be denied admission based on one factor, but it takes appropriate completion of a variety of factors to be admitted.**

Factors to be considered when talking about GPA and lower division major requirements are:

- GPA means transferable grade point average. When applicants compute the GPA, exclude non-transferable courses. The application asks applicants to include "all coursework in your GPA calculation" on the application, but it is re-computed to a UC transferable GPA. I tell my students to put an asterisk (*) next to the GPA on the application, and indicate that it is transferable directly underneath.

- GPA requirements for admission rise and fall depending on the number of qualified students that apply during any particular admission cycle. The GPA that was acceptable last year, may not be this year. Conversely, the non-competitive GPA last year might be acceptable this year.

- Students with lower GPAs, but many lower division major courses completed at the time of application might be more attractive than students with higher GPAs but less lower division major courses completed.

- If the school a student attends does not offer the necessary lower division major coursework, **usually** the student will not be penalized for not having them completed, but it will take longer to graduate after transfer. However, claims like "It's not offered at a convenient time for me," fall on deaf ears. There are other students that **will** make it convenient!

- On the following pages, I have provided the lower division major requirements for the majors that require significant coursework to be completed prior to admission. However, if a major or college is listed on the following pages without the lower division major requirements, I urge students to get on the Worldwide Web and go to: www.assist.org. This site lists lower division major requirements for most UC undergraduate majors and it is updated frequently.

How Does One Determine Which Courses Completed at Another School or College Will Satisfy the Appropriate Lower Division Requirements at the UC Campus that a Student Wants to Transfer into?

There are two major assumptions before I proceed: First, that the college, school, or university where the class was completed meets the accreditation standards discussed in Chapter Three. Second, the course in question was not completed at a California community college. If the student is attending a California community college, the UC has determined the transferability of the course, and in most cases, the specific campus has determined the applicability of the course to lower division major requirements. However, if the course the student is taking has not been designated as equivalent to a lower division major requirement, then follow the procedure below.

There is a recommended procedure that I have used with my students to determine if the course at another institution will be equivalent to a lower division major requirement at the preferred UC campus.

First, find the lower division major requirements at the UC the student wants to attend. Courses can be found either in a specific campus catalog or on specific campus Web page or at www.assist.org.

Second, find the course title and description of the course, or courses, the campus requires of their students to complete for the major.

Third, compare the UC course titles and course descriptions with the course titles and description of the course completed at another institution.

Look for similar or exact words in both the title and description of both courses. Ideally, the courses should have the same number of units. After going through these steps, the student will come to one of three conclusions:

1. There is no match.

2. The match is almost perfect.

3. I'm still not sure!

If conclusion three is reached, there is some more homework. Since we are talking about a lower division major requirement, there is usually a person in the major department that makes decisions about courses from other schools not previously determined to satisfy lower division major requirements. This person could be either a department counselor or sometimes it's the department chair. At this point, the student has two choices:

- Write to the department (e-mail or regular mail), and enclose a course description from the catalog, and ask if their course is equivalent. Either include a self-addressed stamped envelope or a return E-mail address. It would be wise to learn the name of a particular person within the department to whom to direct your correspondence personally.

- Call the department, politely explain your dilemma, and that you need to find the person that determines the applicability of courses to satisfy lower division major requirements. Be willing to fax, E-mail, or regular mail the description. Be willing to submit a syllabus and text book table of contents to help the department determine if your course satisfies their major requirement.

Two points of courtesy:

- Don't make this, "I need to know tomorrow, because I sign up for classes." Plan ahead.

- Be extremely polite. The people with whom students

are dealing are paid to work with, and for, students who currently attend the University, not "wannabees." Say "Please" and "Thank You" often!

I can't stress it enough: The only way to know if you are admissible is to apply. Your particular combination of factors might catch somebody's eye. (Sorry for the rhyme.)

Enhancing Your Attractiveness for Admission Consideration

Berkeley once turned down a 4.0 Engineering transfer student from SMC. When our Transfer Center Director investigated, Berkeley said that he was denied because he had no other extracurricular activities on his application. Does this mean you should fill every box available on the application that indicates you are involved in extracurricular activities? No. If you choose to involve yourself in extracurricular activities, pick two or three activities, and get seriously involved, not peripherally involved. Working 30–40 hours per week and/or raising children count as extracurricular activities. Even if you have the GPA and all the lower division major requirements, the UCs are looking to admit students that are not focused only on academics. Currently, the UC system does not take into consideration race, ethnicity, or gender when making admission decisions.

Berkeley

The Office of Undergraduate Admission and Relations with Schools has a publication titled *Transfer Admission* that is useful.

College of Letters & Science: *VERY IMPORTANT*: 50% of transfer students are admitted with GPAs between 3.5–3.9. The other 50% are considered with other GPAs and other factors like age, campus involvement, employment, outside activities, overcoming particular challenges, having a special talent, family obligations or first-generation college student.

The College of Letters & Science admits students into specific academic divisions, not individual majors. The ranges for GPA admission consideration for students admitted on academic criteria alone are between a 3.5–3.9. Keep in mind the aforementioned 50% "rule." **If a student decides not to apply just because their GPA does not fall into this range, they are making a very flawed decision.**

Since the GPAs are so high in the College of Letters and Science, it is critical that you complete significant lower division coursework in the major. The more lower division coursework completed at the time of application, the more attractive a student is for admission consideration. There are five impacted majors in the College of Letters and Science: Computer Science, Economics, Mass Communication, Political Economy and Industrial Societies, Psychology, and Social Welfare. Even if you are admitted to Berkeley, you must meet the individual screening requirements of these majors after transfer.

Walter A. Haas School of Business: Your application is first reviewed by the University undergraduate admissions office to review for minimum university admissibility. Then the application is sent to the Haas School of Business. The undergraduate office looks for a 3.3 GPA and completion of lower division major requirements and 7 of the nine breadth requirements. A supplemental application to the candidate asking for a professional resume, a letter of recommendation, and two essay samples is mailed to strong candidates. Solid writing skills are critical in order to be a competitive applicant. Although some students are admitted with a 3.3–3.5, most are admitted in the 3.7–4.0 range, but the GPA is not the sole criterion. Completion of all the lower division major requirements and seven of the general education requirements is critical. Lower division major coursework over 5 years old will not be considered as valid. (This does not apply to GE coursework).

The following four (Berkeley) Colleges do not advertise a specific GPA cut-off. Because there are so many academically qualified applicants, the Colleges can wait until the applications are in and look at the totality of prospective students. For example, the essay is a critical factor for a 4.0 Engineering student. Please refer to www.assist.org for detailed information about specific lower division major requirements.

College of Chemistry: Required: One year of General Chemistry (emphasis on the capital "G"; not Chemistry for non-majors.), one year of Calculus, and one course in Calculus-based Physics.

College of Engineering: Complete one year of General Chemistry, five semesters of non-business Calculus, and three semesters of Calculus-based Physics for Physics majors. Additional courses may be required for specific majors in engineering and www.assist.org is the best place to locate those courses and their equivalents.

College of Environmental Design: Maximum of 17 transferable semester units in Design/Architecture/Landscape Architecture. The actual application of these courses towards major requirements will be determined after transfer and a portfolio review.

College of Natural Resources: Complete lower division preparation for the major as listed on www.assist.org.

Davis

The Office of Undergraduate Admissions has a brochure titled *UC Davis Admission Information, 2002–03* that has a section titled "Transfer: Eligibility and Admission" that is helpful.

The appropriate GPA needed to enhance a student's

attractiveness for admission consideration is a 2.8 or higher.

Davis has three undergraduate Colleges: the College of Engineering, the College of Agricultural and Environmental Sciences, and the College of Letters & Science. The Division of Biological Science straddles the College of Agriculture & Environmental Science and College of Letters & Science and offers majors that fall under both Colleges. The key for admission to any of these Biological Science majors is completing lower division coursework in the major. This is what impresses the admission committee.

College of Agricultural & Environmental Sciences: The GPA range is 2.8–3.0 for admission. Also, if you met University Admission requirements by way of your performance in high school (see Appendix "A"), then you can apply with fewer than 60 transferable semester units. There are six majors that require specific course completion before a student is considered for admission:

Biotechnology requires the following courses with an overall GPA of 2.8–3.0, no course lower than a "C", and each sequence requires a minimum 2.5 GPA:

- One year of Calculus
- One year of General Chemistry with labs
- One course in Biology for Biology majors (Not an Introductory course), but one full year is strongly encouraged
- It is strongly recommended to complete one year of Organic Chemistry

Design is a major that requires the submission of a portfolio in February prior to admission (a student must submit an application to the university in the previous month of November). Students are highly encouraged (but not required) to take the following coursework at the community college to insure a smooth transition: drawing, media, color theory, art history, photography, drafting and visual computing.

Fermentation Science requires the following courses completed with a 3.0 or higher with no grade lower than a "C":
• One year of General Chemistry with labs
• One course in Organic Chemistry for majors with a lab
• One Calculus course (not Business Calculus)
• One Calculus based Physics course
• One course in Biology for Biology majors

If the student wants to begin upper division work upon entry into Davis, they should also complete a second semester of Organic Chemistry, Calculus, and Physics.

Landscape Architecture requires a portfolio submission in April (after applying the previous November). Please consult the web site: www.assist.org for lower division major preparation.

Managerial Economics requires the following courses and an an overall 2.8 GPA or above with no grade less than a "C."

  • Microeconomics and Macroeconomics
  • Statistics and two Calculus courses

The Department of Agricultural and Resource Economics will consider only the first repeat of any pre-major course in their petition review. Admission to the major is only determined at the conclusion of the first quarter.

Viticulture and Enology requires the following courses completed with a 3.0 or higher with no grade lower than a "C":

- One year of General Chemistry with labs
- One course in Organic Chemistry for majors with a lab
- One Calculus course (not Business Calculus)
- One Calculus-based Physics course
- One course in Biology for Biology majors

If the student wants to begin upper division work upon entry into Davis, they should also complete a second semester of Organic Chemistry, Calculus, and Physics. Minimum transfer GPA to be competitive is a 2.8–3.0.

College of Engineering: All majors require lower division major preparation completed in Chemistry, Calculus & Physics, with a 2.8–3.0 GPA.

College of Letters & Sciences: There are three majors that have higher selection criteria than the others:

Computer Science requires:

- 2.8–3.0 GPA or higher in all transferable work
- A 3.0 GPA in the following lower division major requirements:
  - Pascal Programming Course
  - Introduction to software development
  - A Computer Science 50 or Electrical & Computer Engineering 70 at Davis
  - One year of Calculus and one course in Linear Algebra

International Relations requires:

- One course in Microeconomics
- One course in Macroeconomics
- One course in World Geography
- One course in History of Western Civilization from 18th Century to the present

- One Political Science course on International Relations

A 3.0 GPA is required in these courses, with an overall 2.8–3.0 GPA in all transferable work.

<u>Psychology</u> requires a student to complete:
- One course in General Psychology
- One Statistics course
- One Research Methods Psychology course (if your school doesn't offer this course, it can be completed after transfer. This course usually has Statistics as a pre-requisite)
- One Biology course designed for a non-biology majors
- One course from:
  - A Physical Anthropology course
  - An Introductory course on Human Heredity
  - An introductory course on Human Physiology
  - One transferable course in Sociology or Cultural Anthropology

A 3.0 GPA is required in these major preparation courses and an overall 2.8–3.0 GPA in all transferable courses.

<u>Division of Biological Sciences:</u> The ten majors in the Biological Sciences require the student to complete the following lower division preparation:
- One year of Calculus with a 2.5 GPA
- One year of General Chemistry with a 2.5 GPA
- One year of General Biology (for Biology Major) with a 2.5 GPA
- One year of Organic Chemistry with a 2.5 GPA
- The overall GPA in all transferable work must be in the range of 2.8–3.0.

Irvine

The Office of Admissions and Relations with Schools has an excellent brochure titled *California Community College Transfer Admission, Selection, and Preparation.*

The approximate GPA needed to enhance your attractiveness for admission consideration is a 2.8. Students have been admitted with 2.4–3.2 at Irvine. There are specific undergraduate academic units at Irvine:

School of the Arts

School of Biological Science

The Henry Samueli School of Engineering

School of Humanities

Department of Information & Computer Science

School of Physical Science

School of Social Ecology

School of Social Science

The following Schools or majors are considered harder to transfer into than others. (A minimum of 3.0 GPA and significant coursework in the specific majors):

<u>**Applied Ecology**</u> requires:

- One year of Biology for majors
- One Course in Molecular Biology
- One Year of Calculus based Physics with lab
- One year of General Chemistry with labs

- One year of Organic Chemistry with labs
- One course in Economics
- One Computer Introduction course that includes programming
- One Calculus course and either another Calculus or Statistics course
- One course in C++
- One course in Ecology and Evolution

School of Biological Science requires:

- One year of Biology for majors
  or
- One course in Botany and one course in Zoology
- One year of General Chemistry with labs
- One year of Organic Chemistry with labs
- One Calculus course and either another Calculus or Statistics course
- One year of Calculus-based Physics
- One course in each of these areas: Ecology & Evolution, Genetics, Biochemistry, and Molecular Biology

Psychology and Social Behavior requires:

- One Introductory Sociology course
- One Introductory Psychology course
- One course in Statistics

Psychology requires:

- One general Psychology course
- One course in C, C++, or Pascal
- One year of Calculus
- Two courses from:
  Anthropology, Economics, Sociology, Linguistics, Political Science

Earth and Environmental Sciences requires:

- Two years of Calculus
- One year of General Chemistry with lab
- One year of Calculus based Physics
- One course in Corchorfortran

Economics requires:

- One course in Microeconomics and Macroeconomics
- One year of Calculus
- One course in C, C++, or Pascal
- Three Introductory Social Science courses in disciplines other than economics

For the Economics Honor Program, complete one course in Linear Algebra.

Chemistry requires:

- One year of General Chemistry with labs
- One year of Organic Chemistry with labs
- One year of Calculus and one course in multi-variable Calculus
- One year of Calculus-based Physics for majors

The Henry Samueli School of Engineering has several majors.

All majors require:

- Two years of Calculus
- One and one half years of Calculus-based Engineering Physics. In addition Aerospace wants one course in General Chemistry with lab and one course in C, C++, or Fortran.

Chemical Engineering wants one year of General Chemistry and course in C, C++, or Fortran.

Civil Engineering wants one year of General Chemistry with labs for majors.

Computer Engineering wants one Chemistry course for majors (not an Intro.), one course in C or C++

Electrical Engineering wants one Chemistry course for majors (not an Intro.)

General Engineering wants one year of General Chemistry with labs for majors. One course in C or C++, or Fortran.

Environmental Engineering wants one year of General Chemistry for majors. One course in Organic Chemistry for majors. One course in C, C++, or Fortran.

Material Science wants one course in C, C++, or Fortran and one year of General Chemistry with labs.

Mechanical Engineering wants one year of General Chemistry for majors. One course in C, C++, or Fortran.

Important:
Some of the Engineering majors recommend completion of certain Engineering courses and Computer Science courses, but these courses are so varied and mostly unavailable at the community colleges, that I chose not to list them. Check www.assist.org to see if your school offers an equivalent course. Consult the UCI publication, *California Community College Transfer Admission, Selection, and Preparation.*

Department of Information and Computer Science wants one year of Calculus. One course in Linear Algebra and one course in Discrete Math. One year of transferable Computer Science courses with programming languages in: C++, Eiffel, or another object-oriented high level language.

Mathematics major requires:

- Two years of Calculus courses (should include Linear Algebra, Differential Equations, and Multivariable Calculus, including the Theorems of Green, Stores, and Gaus.)
- One year of General Chemistry
  or
- One year of Calculus-based Physics for physics majors
- One course in C, C++, or Fortran.
- One additional course in computational methods.

Physics major requires:

- Two years of Calculus courses.
- One and one-half years of Calculus-based Physics for Physics majors.
- One course in C Programming and Numerical Analysis.

Los Angeles

The Office of Undergraduate Admissions and Relations with Schools has a publication titled *Transfer Admission Guide* that is useful.

The College of Letters & Science:

A GPA of 3.3 or higher will make you attractive in the admissions process. Certain majors in the College require higher GPAs:

- Life Science Majors: Requires a 3.4–3.6 (The majors in Life Sciences are Biology; Ecology, Behavior, and Evolution; Marine Biology; Microbiology and Molecular Genetics; Molecular, Cell, and Development Biology;

Neuroscience; Physiological Science; Plant Biology; Psychobiology
- Communication Studies: Requires 3.5 and higher
- All Economics majors: 3.4–3.6
- Sociology: Requires a 3.4–3.6

Political Science and Psychology were on this list for a long time, but, no longer. It is possible, that majors not currently listed will appear next time, or some of the current majors could drop off the list.

College of Letters & Science most selective majors:
Communication Studies
- One course in Mass or Interpersonal Communication
- One course in Principles of Public Speaking
- One course in Communication & Cultural Anthropology
- One course in Introduction to Linguistics
- One transferable course in statistics
- Select three courses from the following menu:
  - One course from Micro-economics, Macro-economics, or Introduction to Political Economy (only one of these three)
  - Introductory Psychology
  - Introductory Sociology
  - Introduction to American Government/Politics

Economics/Business or Economics or Econ-International Area Studies:

Repetition of more than one lower division major course or repetition more than once of any single lower division major course results in automatic denial of admission to the major. "Repetition" means repeating a course for which you have earned a "D", "F", or "No Credit" (NC) in. Getting a "W" (Withdraw) then taking it again is not considered a repetition.

- One course in Micro-economics
- One course in Macro-economics
- One year of Calculus (Same as a Math major takes. Note: Business Calculus, Soft Calculus, or Short Calculus is not acceptable!)
- One course in Statistics (Statistics offered by a Math Department, not other academic departments.)
- One course in English Composition & Literature (This usually is satisfied with a second semester English Composition requirement)

Economics/Business would also like you to complete:

- One course in Elementary Financial Accounting.
- One course in Elementary Managerial Accounting

Economic International Area Studies:

The major doesn't require the English Composition & Literature course, but minimum transfer university admission requirements do require this second course. The major department wants two years of a Foreign Language in the area that the student wishes to concentrate.

Life Science majors:

- One year of Biology for majors with a lab
- One year of General Chemistry for majors with a lab
- One year of Calculus
- One semester of organic Chemistry with lab

A second semester of Organic Chemistry or one year of Calculus-based Physics is strongly recommended.

Sociology:

- One Course in Introductory Sociology
- One course in Statistics
- One course in finite mathematics or calculus

Schools of the Arts & Architecture:
These majors admit students based more on exhibited talent than on grade point average. Auditions, portfolios, and/or evidence of creativity are critical. If students have talent and a minimum 3.0, they can get in. If they are a 4.0 student, and, well, let's say "less talented," they won't get in. If they are below a 3.0, they should make the effort to show their talent to the department that can then request their file directly.

World Arts and Cultures:
The department reviews all applicants. There are additional requirements due in early January:
- Two Letters of Recommendation
- Extra Questionnaire: "Why do you want this major?"
- Supplementary: Research Paper, Videotape, Photos

School of Theater, Film, & Television:
There are only two majors in this School: **Film & Television** and **Theater**. A 3.0 GPA is considered necessary for admission consideration.

Theater: Requires an audition.

Film and Television has a writing requirement for admission. A student will need to submit a critical essay and a creative writing sample after they have passed the initial screening by the Admissions Office. There are no specific courses for the student to complete that would enhance their attractiveness for admission. Admission consideration is heavily weighted on the writing samples.

The Henry Samueli School of Engineering and Applied Science:

The lower division major requirements a student should complete prior to transfer are:

- Two years of Calculus including differential equations and Linear Algebra
- Calculus-based Physics that includes mechanics, electricity and magnetism, waves, sound, heat and Modern Physics
- One year of General Chemistry: note: Computer Science and Engineering students only need one General Chemistry course. Computer Science students don't need any chemistry.
- Students should learn either Fortran, Pascal, C Programming, or C++. Computer-related majors require C++.

Average GPA For 2000 Admission		Lowest GPA Accepted 2000
3.50	Aerospace	3.34
3.78	Chemical	3.33
3.74	Civil	3.33
3.82	Computer Science	3.56
3.82	Computer Science	3.40
	& Engineering	3.24
3.76	Electrical	3.71
3.83	Materials	3.32
3.69	Mechanical	3.32

If when a student applies, they indicate a second choice major, they might be considered in that second choice if not admitted for their first choice major.

Riverside

The office of Admissions-Information for Prospective Students/Relations with Schools has a publication titled *Undergraduate Admission Requirements: Admission as a Transfer* that is helpful.

Riverside will accept students who are minimally eligible and have a 2.4 GPA. However, they warn that Biology, Biological Sciences, Biochemistry, Business Administration, Engineering (Chemical, Computer, Electrical, Environmental, and Mechanical Engineering), and majors in the College of Natural & Agricultural Sciences need significant lower division major coursework to be competitive for admission and a higher GPA.

Riverside has three Colleges. The College of Humanities, Arts, & Social Science, the College of Natural & Agricultural Sciences, and the Marlon and Rosemary Bourns College of Engineering.

College of Humanities, Theatres, Arts, and Social Sciences
Business Administration:
- A minimum 2.5 GPA
- Complete seven of the following ten lower division courses:

  - Microeconomics
  - Macroeconomics
  - Intro to Business
  - Principles of Accounting I, II
  - Intro to computing
  - Calculus for Business
  - Statistics for Business
  - Applied Matrix Algebra
    - Psychology Methods: Research Procedures

- Complete the IGETC

College of Natural & Agricultural Science:
Complete three of the five transferable year-long sequences (as they relate to a student's major per the catalog) from the following choices with an overall 2.7 GPA:

- One year of General Chemistry for majors
- One year of Calculus
- One year of Biology for majors
- One year of Calculus-based Physics
- One year of Organic Chemistry

Biochemistry majors must complete General Calculus and Chemistry for admission. Biology and Biological Science majors must complete Calculus and Chemistry majors. Majors must complete Calculus and General Chemistry to graduate. All sequences must be completed.

School of Engineering:

To ensure a timely graduation and smooth admission:
- Two years of Calculus
- One year of Physics for Engineers
- One year of English Composition
- One year of college Chemistry (note: Computer Science majors need only one chemistry course)

Computer Science majors should complete two programming courses prior to transfer (C or C++).

San Diego

The Office of Admissions and Relations with Schools has a publication titled *The Transfer Advantage* that is useful.

San Diego is organized somewhat differently than the other campuses. There are five Colleges, and you can enroll in any college and major in any major. Each of San Diego's five colleges, aside from their names and residential grouping, has a different general education pattern. Three of the five colleges accept IGETC. If a Revelle or Roosevelt student completes IGETC, additional lower division general education courses must be completed after transfer.

San Diego requires transfer applicants to have a minimum 2.8 GPA at the time of application for admission consideration.

If you apply for Fall admission, they will use your grades from the Fall for admission consideration. **It is important** to complete as many lower division major requirements as possible to assist with a smooth transfer and a timely graduation.

<u>Biological Science</u> majors will be looking for the following courses to be completed by transfer students:
- One year of Biology for Biology majors
- One year of General Chemistry
- One year of Calculus-based Physics
- One year of Calculus

<u>Human Development</u> majors should complete all of the following courses for maximum admission consideration:
- One statistics course
- One calculus course
- Two courses in Biological Sciences for Biology majors
- One general introductory computer or programming course
- Two introductory social science courses

If a student is trying to use a non-community college transferable course, please contact the Human Development Department to determine applicability at 858-534-9919.

Santa Barbara

Admissions and Outreach Services has a publication titled, *Transfer Information, 2002-2003* that is helpful.

Santa Barbara has three Colleges: The College of Creative Studies, The College of Engineering, and the College of Letters & Science. The minimum GPA "cushion to insure competitiveness is 2.7+." The College of Engineering, the major of Computer Science, and the College of Creative Studies are more competitive. Therefore, the higher your GPA and more lower division preparation completed, the more likely you will be admitted. The College of Creative Studies requires an additional application that will be mailed to you after your initial application.

There are seven other impacted majors that have additional academic performance requirements after you get admitted. For instance, if you apply to the Economics major, and get admitted, your status is as a pre-Economics major. After you arrive, you must complete your remaining lower division, or if those are completed, some upper division courses, with a 2.7 GPA. The other similar majors are:

> **Business Economics**
>
> **Communication**
>
> **Law & Society**
>
> **Mathematics**
>
> **Political Science**
>
> **Psychology**
>
> **Sociology**

Here are the lower division major requirements that you should try to complete prior to transfer:

Business Economics requires:

- Microeconomics
- Macroeconomics
- Two courses in Financial Accounting
- Two courses in Calculus (Calculus for Life or Social Science is acceptable)
- Statistics with Economics and Business Application

Biopsychology requires:

- One Introductory course in Psychology

- One year of Biology (for Biology majors)
- One year of General Chemistry
- One year of organic Chemistry
- One year of calculus-based physics
- One year of calculus
- One statistics course

Communications requires:

- Introduction in Communication
- Communication Research Methods
- Theories of Communication
- A transferable statistics course

Law and Society requires:

- Introduction course on Law and Society
- Socio-Legal Research Methods with a lab
- One course on American Government and Politics
- Introductory Cultural Anthropology
- A course on Social Organization
- A transferable Statistics course

Mathematics requires:

- Two years of Calculus
- One course in Calculus-based Physics
- One course Introduction to Computer Programming

Political Science requires:

- Political Ideas in the Modern World
- Introduction to Comparative Politics
- Introduction to International Relations
- American Government and Politics
- Microeconomics and Macroeconomics
- One year of The History of Western Civilization

(For the **Political Science International Relations** major add:

Two years of a foreign language to the above requirements.)
(For the **Political Science Public Service** major add: One year of Financial Accounting to the above requirements.)

Psychology requires:

- One General Psychology course
- One transferable Statistics course
- Introduction to Experimental Psychology
- One course in Calculus for Social or Life Science majors or equivalent
- One course from two of the following five areas:
  - <u>Area 1</u>: Concepts of Biology or Contemporary Natural Science in Biology
  - <u>Area 2</u>: Human Anatomy or Human Development and Reproductive Physiology
  - <u>Area 3</u>:Introductory Chemistry or Contemporary Natural Science in Physics
  - <u>Area 4</u>: A survey Physics course for non-majors or Contemporary Natural Science in Physics
  - <u>Area 5</u>: An Introductory course in Computer Programming and Organization

Sociology requires:

- One course in Social Organization
- One course on Social Psychology
- Introduction to Quantitative Sociological Studies or Statistics
- One course in Sociological Research Traditions
- A course focusing on the American people from the Civil War to the Present
- Two courses from the following list:
  Cultural Anthropology; Issues in the History of Public

Policy; The American People: From Colonial to Jacksonian Period; Macroeconomics; Political Ideas in the Modern World; Comparative Politics; International Relations; American Government and Politics; Introductory Psychology; Environmental Studies about the Social or Physical Environment; Human Geography; Philosophical Critical Thinking; Philosophical Ethics, or Biomedical Ethics

Selective Majors

<u>Computer Science</u> requires:

- One year of Calculus for math and engineering students
- Calculus based course in Linear Algebra, Differential Equations, and Discrete Probability
- Programming courses in JAVA (preferred), C++, Assembly Language for the B.S., One year of Calculus-based Physics or General Chemistry with lab.
- Two semesters of calculus-based physics

<u>Engineering</u> requires:

- Same as above
- Same as above but Delete Discrete.
- Three semesters of Calculus based Physics
- A year of General Chemistry
- Programming in C Language, Circuits, and Devices
- Additional coursework specific to the major per the catalog

<u>College of Creative Studies</u> require a supplementary application that is looking for outstanding academic and personal achievement, special talent, and capacity for excellence in either Art, Biology, Chemistry, Computer Science, Literature, Mathematics, Music Theory and Composition, or Physics.

<u>Biological Science</u> requires:

- A 2.7 GPA in science and math lower division major listed below.
  - One year of General Chemistry
  - One year of Calculus
  - One year of Biology for Biology majors
  - One year of Physics

For admissions, a student only needs General Chemistry and one of the other three sequences, but to graduate in a more timely manner, a student should complete as much as possible.

Santa Cruz

The Office of Admissions has a publication titled *Transfer and Admission and Selection Guide.*

There are eight different colleges at Santa Cruz, but they are not oriented toward any specific major. You can be in any of the colleges and major in whatever Santa Cruz offers. What differentiates the colleges from one another is course requirements for entering freshmen. Transfer students with 30 or more transferable semester units are not required to satisfy these freshman requirements. Santa Cruz is looking for a 2.4 GPA, but Psychology and Environmental Studies, require a higher GPA to be competitive and Art requires a Portfolio Review.

<u>Art</u> requires:

A student must complete three lower division studio courses and submit 15–20 slides or photographs or video on a website of their work prior to admission.

<u>Environmental Studies</u> requires one transferable course in the following areas:

- Statistics
- Precalculus

- One course in Micro- or Macro Economics
- One Introductory course in National or International Politics or Political theory
- Ethics or Cultural Anthropology or Introductory Sociology
- General Chemistry
- Principles of Ecology

Psychology requires:

- A 3.0 GPA and a 3.1 GPA in all Psychology courses.
- One Introductory Psychology course
- One Introductory Psychology Statistics or Mathematical Statistics course
- One research methods in Psychology course and a research methods laboratory
- An Introductory course in Developmental Psychology
- An Introductory course in Social Psychology*
- An Introductory course in Personality Psychology*
- An Introductory course in Psychobiology *

*These courses are not required to transfer may be prerequisites for upper division courseworks.

There are two **minors** that are considered impacted and difficult to get into:

- Creative Writing minor in the English major
- Production minor in the Film and Video major

Chapter
Five

General Education

Before I talk specifically about general education (GE) requirements, I want to give you the context of where the GEs fit into the baccalaureate degree.

A degree is composed of three parts: 1. major requirements; 2. general education requirements; and 3. electives. Major requirements have two components: lower division courses and upper division courses. Lower division courses are broad survey courses, like: "The History of Western Civilization." Upper division courses are more specific, like: "The History of the Roman Empire - the First 400 Years." General education courses, GEs, are a combination of courses, either upper or lower division, that introduce the student to a broad array of courses in disciplines usually not related to the declared major of the student. Electives are the courses needed to complete the minimum amount of units for graduation. The simplistic formula for a degree looks like this:

Major requirement units + GE units + Elective Units = Minimum Units to graduate (usually, 120 semester units or 180 quarter units)

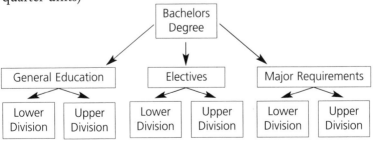

For each school or college, on each of the UC campuses, there is a different set of courses that will satisfy the general education requirements (Other names for this requirement are: breadth, core, or general requirements; I will use "GE" from this point for simplicity.) For example, UCLA students in the College of Letters and Science follow a different set of GE requirements from UCLA students in the School of Theater, Film, and Television.

In 1991, the California Community Colleges (CCC) and the University of California (UC) and the California State University (CSU) systems created the Intersegmental General Education Transfer Curriculum (IGETC–pronounced "I-get-see".) By completing the IGETC completely prior to transfer, a student has completed the lower division general education requirements for all of the UCs in each of their respective schools and colleges. The following exceptions are:

- Haas School of Business at Berkeley
- College of Environmental Design at Berkeley
- The Marlan and Rosemary Bourns College of Engineering at Riverside
- Eleanor Roosevelt College at San Diego*
- Revelle College at San Diego*
- College of Agricultural and Natural Sciences at Riverside

*At San Diego, you can study any major in any of the five colleges. Therefore, you can enter one of the other three colleges and complete the IGETC.

To complete the specific GE for any of the above mentioned schools or colleges, I refer you to ASSIST at www.asist.org to find the courses necessary to complete the colleges' specific GE pattern.

The UC publication *Answers for Transfers*, the IGETC is not an admission requirement. However, completing the lower division breadth/ general education requirement. Whether through the IGETC or the campus specific requirement may improve a transfer applicants chances for admission to a competitive campus and/or program." Therefore, my advice to you is based on four years of counseling transfer students in the College of Letters & Science at UCLA: <u>Finish your general education requirements</u>. It may not always be an admission requirement, but if it is completed, you are more likely to graduate in a timely manner. **<u>Do not</u>** complete IGETC in lieu of the lower division major preparation. You should try to satisfy both if you want to graduate in a timely manner.

You should be aware of specific rules governing the IGETC:

- You must completely finish the IGETC and submit proof of completion prior to your arrival on the UC campus that admits you. Some campuses don't require the official certification in hand prior to beginning your first class, **but** it's better to be safe than sorry.

- Certification can be done only at a California Community College.

- All courses must be completed with a "C" or better. If your school allows   courses to be graded on a "Credit/ No Credit" or "Pass/No Pass" basis, you can choose this grading option and apply it on IGETC. However, your school's definition of "Credit" or "Pass" must be equivalent to a "C" or better (not "C-" or lower!)

- You can use courses from other non-CCC accredited institutions as long as the following guidelines are observed:

  - Non-laboratory courses must be a minimum of 3 semester units or 4 quarter units.
  - Laboratory courses used to satisfy science requirements

must have a minimum of 4 semester units or 5 quarter units of credit.

- Courses from other institutions may be applied to IGETC as long as the certifying California Community College teaches an equivalent course that is on their approved IGETC list.

- You cannot use coursework from a foreign university on IGETC.

For additional information about IGETC guidelines, please check the following Web site:

www.ucop.edu/pathways/infoctr/IGETC_index.html/.

Under rare circumstances, students can complete one or two courses of the IGETC after they transfer. The missing courses can only be in areas 3,4, or 5 (or foreign language for the UC). The rare circumstances must be verifiable hardships, like illness, courses cancelled, or increased work hours. The community college determines if a student qualifies for IGETC After Transfer, and sends the certification to the university. Officials at the university then determine the appropriate courses a student needs to complete the IGETC. The IGETC must be completed within one year after transfer.

IGETC Subject and Unit Requirements for the UC

ENGLISH COMMUNICATION: One course in English composition and one course in Critical thinking/English composition. **The second course must be completed at a CCC.**	2 Courses Required	6 Semester Units **or** 8–10 Quarter Units
MATHEMATICAL CONCEPTS AND QUANTITATIVE REASONING: (The course must have Intermediate Algebra or higher as a pre-requisite)	1 Course Required	3 or more Semester Units **or** 12–15 Quarter Units
ARTS AND HUMANITIES: Three courses with at least one from the Arts and one from the Humanities.	3 Courses Required	9 Semester Units **or** 12–15 Quarter Units
SOCIAL AND BEHAVIORAL SCIENCES: Three courses from at least two disciplines, or an interdisciplinary sequence.	3 Courses Required	9 Semester Units **or** 12–15 Quarter Units
PHYSICAL AND BIOLOGICAL SCIENCES: One physical science course and biological science course and one of the two with lab.	2 Courses Required	7–9 Semester Units **or** 9–12 Quarter Units
LANGUAGE OTHER THAN ENGLISH: Proficiency equivalent to two years of high school in the same language	Proficiency Proficiency is determined by the California Community College that certifies the completion of the IGETC	

Chapter Six

How About Getting Admitted with An Easier Major, Then Switching When I Get There?

Sometimes you can do it, sometimes you can't. One of my responsibilities at UCLA was to meet with transfer students at Orientation who wanted to change their major into or within the College of Letters & Science. My decision to allow them to change their major was not arbitrary, but very objective. The College of Letters & Science at UCLA has a non-negotiable unit ceiling. A unit ceiling means a student must complete degree requirements without exceeding a specific number of units. So, I added up the units completed, and units needed to graduate. If the total didn't go over the maximum number of units allowed, the student didn't violate the unit-ceiling requirement. The student was also required to satisfy major requirements, which could be GPA requirements in the lower division major courses or completing certain courses before you reached a certain total number of units. If all of these requirements were satisfied, a student was allowed to change their major.

I have contacted the various schools and colleges at each of the campuses and noted their responses to the question "What are the parameters for changing your major, when starting as a transfer student?" Keep in mind that these are the general policies for the schools and colleges. Each major at each school might have additional requirements. And even though it may be possible, it could be extremely rare! I have discovered that sometimes these additional requirements are not published in the school's catalog, nor are the UC Outreach staff versed in the rules of changing majors. And, of course, schools can change these policies. The individual major and/or college can inform you of these policies and the likelihood of your change being accepted.

Berkeley:

Haas School of Business:

Once a transfer student arrives at Berkeley, they must complete their Fall semester, then apply to the school in the Spring. A student's competition for admission is other Berkeley students. It is essential that a student should complete their pre-major coursework and more than half of their general education requirement to be competitive. Preferably, all general education coursework should be completed. Rarely does a transfer student get a favorable result.

College of Chemistry:

Complete Fall semester coursework and submit an application to the Dean of the College of Chemistry at the end of the Fall semester. The College of Chemistry admits on the merit of the student. It does not have a unit restriction for admission, but completion of courses listed in Chapter 4 is extremely important.

College of Engineering:

It is "highly unlikely" that a student could switch into Engineering, but "it has been done." The general rule is that a student must be able to complete all the requirements necessary to <u>graduate</u> in five semesters from the time they enter the

University. After they arrive at Berkeley, they must submit a petition to the College of Engineering by February 15th. The application is reviewed by the Engineering faculty. If the faculty likes the student's demonstrated ability, the student's petition is forwarded to the Dean. The Dean reviews the request to see if the student can get the classes they need to complete the graduation requirement by the above specified time. Students admitted in junior standing directly into the College of Engineering are not allowed to change their major.

College of Letters & Science:

Students are allowed to change majors as long as the department is willing to accept the student. Computer Science, Economics, Mass Communication, Psychology, Political Economy of Industrial Societies have high admission standards. Music and Molecular/Cell Biology have a lot of lower division major requirements. Therefore, it is very important to meet with department advisors to discuss the options available to a student.

The College of Letters and Science has a unit ceiling rule. Once a student has completed more than 130 semester units, they will not be allowed to enroll in any more classes. So, if a student has 129 semester units, they need to complete their remaining requirements in the next term!

College of Environmental Design:

To get into this College, a student must have completed:

- One year of Calculus
- One semester of Calculus-based Physics
- One course in Introduction to Environmental Design
- One course in Introductory Drawing
- One course in Introductory Design

You must also be able to complete the major without exceeding 130 semester units.

College of Natural Resources:

They must satisfy the remaining lower division preparation in the specific major to get into the College of Natural Resources. Bear in mind, a student might still need to make some progress in their original college as well. Sometime in the second semester, a student formally applies to the College of Natural Resources. There is no strict unit maximum.

Davis

"Except under unusual circumstance, no change of major will be permitted after you attain senior standing (135 quarter units)." (page 61, 2001/02 Catalog)

You must consult with the individual academic unit to determine the viability of changing your major. Simply stated, changing a major after transfer is never easy, and will usually extend the time a student will take to graduate. By investigating a major thoroughly prior to transfer, a student may not need to do this.

Irvine

Irvine has nine separate undergraduate academic units called schools and departments. Each school or department has a set of majors unique to that individual academic unit. If a student wants to change their major after transferring from one academic unit to another, they must schedule an appointment and go to the school's department into which that they want to switch. The ideal time to do this is immediately during their first quarter. Permission to change their major is determined on a case-by-case basis. UCI does not have a unit ceiling requiring you to complete all requirements by a maximum amount of units.

Los Angeles

College of Letters & Science:

If a student can complete the lower division major requirements, grade admission requirements and upper division major coursework before completing 216 quarter units, they are allowed to change their major, as long as they also complete the criteria of the individual major that they want to change into. For example, the UCLA Catalog states the Psychology department requires that a student complete all lower division major requirements with a 2.3 GPA and no grade lower than a C- by the time the student has completed 110 quarter units.

School of Engineering & Applied Science:

The first consideration by the School is to determine whether the student would have met minimum criteria for admission to the major if the student had applied to this major on the initial application as a first choice.

Second, the college asks "Would admitting the student to the major in the middle of Fall preclude the student from attending school in the Winter & Spring?" Since some upper division major courses are taught in sequences that start in Fall, and if the student misses the Fall courses, they must wait until next Fall to start the sequence. Most students who want to get into Computer Science or Engineering & Computer Science cannot get in because it is so competitive. They are referred to the Math & Computer Science or Cybernetics major in the College of Letters & Science as an alternate major.

School of Art & Architecture:

If a student wants to change into one of the undergraduate majors in this school, they must try to make that decision in the first quarter. Many majors present courses in a sequence, meaning that Part 1 is taught only in Fall, Part 2 taught only in Winter and Part 3 taught only in Spring. Admission is based on portfolio, or audition, and the availability of space in the major. A student is also required to complete all of their requirements to graduate by the time they have completed 216 quarter units.

School of Theater, Film, & Television:

The Theater & Film/Television majors are the only two in this College and will consider petitions to switch over after a student transfers. The College accepts petitions in the Spring quarter, and if they are admitted, they would begin their coursework the following Fall. However, students that have completed 135 quarter units at the time of application would not be considered for admission to either major. Their best shot (and it is still a long shot!), aside from applying directly into the major, would be to transfer in Winter into the College of Letters & Science, then apply to either Film or Theater for the Fall. The College of Letters and Science accepts applications for the Winter. The Schools of Theater, Film & Television do not accept applications for transfer admission in the Winter.

Riverside

A student must be able to complete all of their requirements to graduate by the time they have completed 216 quarter units.

"After having credit for 216 quarter (sic) units, students are not permitted to continue except in cases approved by the Associate Dean in which specific academic or professional reasons are involved."–2001/02 Catalog

This is a University-wide policy. A student transferring in with 60 UC transferable semester units (i.e., 90 quarter units), must be able to finish all of their degree requirements in the remaining 126 quarter units.

San Diego

Changing majors at UCSD can be tricky since they adhere to a strict unit ceiling. A student may not register for more classes after they have exceeded 200 quarter units. Students majoring in Engineering are allowed up to 240 quarter units in Revelle and Roosevelt Colleges, and 230 quarter units if they are Engineering students in Muir, Marshall, or Warren College.

Santa Barbara

College of Creative Studies:

This college accepts transfer applications from other UCSB academic units at any time. Two letters of recommendation are required for most majors, in addition to examples of your artistic endeavors—art, literature, or music. No specific GPA is required. Students should expect to complete at least 6 quarters in this college to graduate. (2001–02 UCSB Catalog, Pg. 59)

Engineering:

"Students who have completed more than 105 quarter units will not be considered for a change of major in engineering or computer science unless they can demonstrate that they will be able to complete all the degree requirements for the proposed program without exceeding 195 quarter (sic) units." (UCSB General Catalog ,2001–02, Page 61)

The College of Engineering will consider a change into Chemical, Electrical, and Mechanical Engineering if:

- The following courses are completed:
  - Two courses in Calculus
  - Two courses in General Chemistry w/ labs
  - Two courses in Engineering equivalent to UCSB's
    - Engineering 1A & 1B or Engineering 2A & 2B
      or
    - One course equivalent to Computer Science 5FO (Fortran)

- One course in Calculus-based Physics (for Physics majors)
- Complete 30 quarter units at UCSB before applying
- Apply during the first four weeks of the Spring quarter. Selection is competitive and is based on the student's UC GPA and lower division major coursework completed.

Students wanting to major in Computer Science must complete 16 quarter units of lower division Computer Science major requirements (8 of those 16 units must be in Computer Science) with a 3.0 GPA in all lower division major requirements. With these criteria met, you can be declared a pre-Computer Science major.

Upon completion of all lower division Computer Science major requirements and Probability & Statistics 120A (an upper division course) with UC GPA minimum of 2.75 in those courses, a student must petition, and will be admitted into the Computer Science major.

College of Letters & Science:

A student wishing to get into a major in this College must complete all the lower division major requirements of the major you intend to enter and file a petition with the Chair of the department and the Provost of the College of Letters & Science. Here's the **big** warning:

"Students who contemplate a change of major relatively late in their academic careers should note that the change may not be approved if it becomes clear that they will need to complete more than 200 quarter (sic) units in order to fulfill all degree requirements." (UCSD 2001/02 Catalog, Page 118)

You can petition to exceed the 200 quarter unit maximum, and petitions are considered on a case-by-case basis.

Remember, if a student is transferring in with 60 transferable semester units, they already have 90 quarter units. Therefore, if a student wants to switch into a non-Engineering major, they must be able to complete that major within 110 quarter units at UCSD. (2001/02 UCSD Catalog, Pg. 64)

Santa Cruz

At Santa Cruz the decision to allow a student into a major is governed by the respective department. Some majors have limited space, specific requirements, or want the student to have completed significant lower division major coursework. The 2001/02 catalog, page 34 states:

> "Junior transfer students must file a study plan and declare a major during their second quarter at UCSC by the deadline printed in the Academic and Administrative Calendar in the Schedule of Classes."

The question is "How much wiggle-room exists in that policy?" It depends on the particular major department. Some could point to the policy and say, "That's the policy," others might bend the policy in a favorable direction for the student.

In conclusion, trying to "get in the back door" with one major, and then switching when a student gets there is risky, and subject to a variety of rules and regulations. Community college counselors and UC Outreach are not well versed regarding the rules and regulations surrounding changing majors after transfer. When attempting to discern the likelihood of changing majors after transfer with university personnel that have the authority to allow any changes after transfer, the student should document all conversations and get as much documentation in writing as is possible.

Chapter
Seven

Applying, Appealing and Guaranteed Admission Programs

All UC campuses accept applications for Fall admission during the preceding month of November. The application envelope must be postmarked with any date in November. You don't get extra points for having it post-marked November 1st vs. November 30th. Historically, after November 30, most UC campuses do not accept applications. Berkeley, Los Angeles, and San Diego did not accept applications after November 30, 2001. Santa Cruz, Santa Barbara, Irvine, and Riverside accepted applications after the November 30th deadline. For maximum consideration, the application must be postmarked before the end of November.

Fortunately, it is not necessary to have all 60 UC transferable semester units completed at the time of application. For maximum consideration and selection, a student should have as much lower division major coursework completed as possible. Even if a student hasn't met the above criteria prior to applying, they should still apply. I never counsel someone to not apply. Every year, there is at least one student I counsel that I think, "This one doesn't have a snowball's chance in Hell!" In May, that same student wanders back into my office to say, "Thanks" because they were, indeed, accepted at a campus.

The UC application advertises dates for submitting applications for either Winter or Spring admission. Each campus has different policies regarding admission in Winter or Spring. For example, UC Berkeley and UCLA do not accept any applications for Spring. Anybody can go to Summer School at UC, as long as you pay the hefty fees. Attending a UC in Summer does not mean automatic admission the following Fall, nor does it give you any advantage.

Berkeley

The Berkeley campus is on the semester system. Berkeley accepts students in the Spring semester <u>only</u> if they applied for Fall. Occasionally, Berkeley wants some students for whom they have no space in the Fall, so, they offer them Spring admission. Courses in progress at the time of application <u>will be</u> considered for admission. Remember, if a student applies in November, they haven't seen the Fall grades! Note: Berkeley does not allow a student to apply to a second choice or alternate major.

Davis

Davis will consider applications for admission in Winter. A student can appeal for Davis to accept an application in Spring, if they can prove they have completed all lower division requirements and all general education requirements at the community college or if they have a TAA (Transfer Admission Agreement). Call the Admissions Office to ask about the application procedure. Davis <u>will</u> use grades from courses in progress at the time of application for admission consideration, but they <u>will not</u> admit the student to a second choice major.

Irvine

Irvine will accept application for Winter quarter. Irvine will consider appeals <u>directly</u> to the Admissions Office for the

Spring quarter, but a student must make the case that admission is justified on sound, educational criteria. Irvine <u>will</u> consider an alternate major on the application, but will only consider courses in progress at the time of application if submitted with an appeal (personally, I would send the Fall grades as soon as they are available!)

Los Angeles

UCLA accepts applications for the Winter quarter in the School of Engineering and College of Letters & Science, except for the Communications Studies major and all the Economics majors. A student must apply the previous July. They do not accept Winter applicants for the School of Theater, Motion Picture & Television, or the School of Arts & Architecture. UCLA considers grades from classes in progress at the time of application for Fall or Winter admission. Only the School of Engineering will consider a second choice or alternative major for admission consideration when the student lists one on the application. UCLA does not accept any applications for the Spring quarter.

Riverside

Riverside accepts applications for all terms, but accepts Engineering, Biochemistry, and Chemistry students only in the Fall. Biological Sciences and Biology majors are only accepted in the Fall and Winter. International applicants must file during the priority filing periods (November for Fall, July for winter and October for Spring). Riverside uses grades from courses in progress at the time of application if they are sent and they will look at alternate majors on the application.

San Diego

San Diego will only accept students for Winter and Spring if they are participating in the UCSD Transfer Admissions

Guarantee Program. San Diego <u>will not</u> consider second choice majors, but they will use grades from courses in progress at the time of application to determine admissibility.

Santa Barbara

Accepts Junior transfers for Winter, except in Computer Science, Engineering majors, and International applicants.

Santa Cruz

Santa Cruz has accepted applications for Winter but not for Spring. They <u>will not</u> consider students for second choice major, but they <u>will</u> look at Fall grades for admission consideration.

The Application Personal Statement

The essay is one of the most important parts of your application. It is harder than it appears. Entire books have been written about how to write a college application essay. Students that use these books end up with essays similar to those used as examples in the book, so says many of the UC Admission staff that read the essays. The UC personal statement, is the one place where a student gets to "speak" to the admissions people. I have heard various UC Admissions Directors give a workshop on the personal statement, and their suggestions were very helpful and precise:

1. Write to the prompt. There are usually two or three prompts, or ideas, that a student can write about. Too many personal statements wander away from those prompts, so **stay focused**.

2. Write your own essay. A format copied from other successful essays is easy for Admission readers to spot and is usually met by a negative first impression from the reader.

3. Write in your own voice. Using "I" is perfectly acceptable. This personal statement is taking the place of an interview, and the reader is trying to find out who the student is.

4. Do not mistake a list for an essay. This is the biggest problem I see in essays. Some students feel the need to list all their accomplishments in the essay, even if they have listed the information on the application. Write with thought and insight and show the reader the person behind the grades.

5. Read the essay aloud to yourself first, then to someone with a critical ear. Parents, boyfriends, girlfriends, and spouses are not usually the best to give helpful criticism. Teachers, counselors and students currently at the institution you want to attend can be helpful. Listen to their criticism with a critical ear yourself. It's okay to make recommended changes, but don't lose the soul of your essay.

6. Don't try to be wildly funny.

7. Avoid clichés and trite statements, such as "I want to be a doctor so I can help people" or "Going to college was a struggle for me." Your desire to "help people" can be described in terms of a personal experience where you helped people. Your "struggle" can be described by the balancing act you had between work, family obligations and/or health issues. Show, don't tell.

8. Proofread and edit. Treat this as a "personal manifesto" you would be proud to have published in *The New York Times*.

Guaranteed Admission Programs

You have probably heard about admission programs offered at the California Community Colleges that "guarantee" that you will get into the University of California. But, like any "guarantee" there are, however, a lot of exceptions, or caveats, and few of the programs are truly "guaranteed." Those that are considered such, might be restricted to certain majors or might require a student to attend a specific community college (see Appendix "B".) For example, the UCLA Transfer Alliance Program (TAP) offers "<u>priority consideration</u> for admission" for applicants at 22 California community colleges, but only to the College of Letters & Science with the exception of the Communication Studies major. In the Fall semester of 2000, UCLA accepted 587 students from Santa Monica College, and only 70 were in the Transfer Alliance Program. That's only 12%. The other 88% earned their admission doing well academically and completing all the other transfer requirements previously mentioned in this book. If a student performs well and completes the transfer admission requirements, the application will receive favorable consideration.

Let's look at each of the campuses and their transfer programs. A student may wish to consider enrolling in the honors program at the community college, if there is one. By doing so, the student will enhance their application and better prepare themselves for academic success <u>after transfer</u> due to the rigorous honors courses at their community college.

Berkeley

The Cooperative Admission Program (CAP) is offered <u>only</u> to students who apply to Berkeley for freshman admission, are UC-eligible out of high school but are not admitted as freshman. They must also meet the following criteria:

<u>**Letters & Science**</u>: (This one sounds good, but read the fine print!) All students that are UC-eligible who are not admitted may gain admission if they: (Here comes the fine print!)

- Complete 60 transferable units
- Complete either the College Basic Breadth requirements

in Foreign Language, Quantitative Reasoning, and/or
Reading & Composition
> or
>
> IGETC

- Complete Pre-Requisites in the Major
- Earn a specified GPA (3.3 for Fall 2002)
- Attend one of the 39 specified community colleges (See
  Appendix "B")

You can see that the CAP requirements are not demonstrably different than the general transfer admission requirements.

College of Environmental Design:

The faculty from this college will review the application to CAP and determine if the student can participate. Selection is based on high school performance and a student must have applied previously direct from high school. Then, a student must complete 60 UC transferable units with a 3.0 GPA and all lower division major requirements and attend one of 10 specific California community colleges (see Appendix "B".)

College of Natural Resources:

<u>All</u> UC-eligible freshman applicants who are not admitted are offered the CAP option. A student must complete 60 UC transferable units with a 3.0 GPA at one of seven specific California community colleges (I would strongly recommend a student complete as many lower division major requirements as possible, too). (See Appendix "B".)

College of Engineering:

The College of Engineering selects CAP students from the freshman that apply and requires them to complete a minimum of 60 transferable semester units with specific lower division major requirements completed with a 3.5 GPA at one of 19 specific California community colleges.

Davis

Davis offers Transfer Admission Agreements (TAA). This agreement is drafted by a community college counselor and the student.

> "The agreement lists the courses the student will complete at community college, with emphasis on courses required for admission, major pre-requisites and breadth requirements. Students who comply with the agreement and apply for admission on time during the appropriate filing period are guaranteed admission to a specific quarter in advance. This option is available in all majors except landscape architecture and design."
>
> 2002–03 UC Answers for Transfers

The TAA must be reviewed by a UC Davis admissions representative and the student must attend one of 45 specific California Community Colleges. (See Appendix "B")

Irvine

PAIF stands for "Preliminary Admission in the Field." This programs offers on-the-spot admission to highly qualified students. Students meet with a UCI representative, on their campus or at UCI, for an on-site review of their qualifications. Qualified applicants offered preliminary provisional admissions are given recommendations for coursework that must be completed prior to transfer.

The Community College Honors Transfer Program requires that the student attend one of 28 specific California community colleges (see Appendix "B"), enroll in and successfully complete the honors program. Each community college has different requirements for its honors program. If a student successfully completes this program, the student will receive "priority admission consideration" (but no guarantees!).

Los Angeles

The Transfer Alliance Program (TAP) at UCLA requires a student to meet general university transfer admission requirements and complete the honors program at one of 25 specific community colleges (see Appendix "B"). This program offers "priority consideration" for admission only to the College of Letters & Science (except the Communication Studies major). No guarantees here!

Riverside

The Transfer Admission Guarantee (TAG) program is a contract set-up between the student and UCR. There are no contracts for students wishing to apply to the College of Engineering. To set up a contract, you must call the Transfer and Re-entry Services Offices at (909) 787-5307 or send an e-mail to: transfer@pop.ucr.edu.

This program is available to students that have attended only a California Community College. If a student has attended any other college or university, the student would not be eligible for the program.

San Diego

The Transfer Admission Guarantee program (TAG) requires a student to complete the UC minimum admission requirement, earn a specified GPA, complete specific TAG core courses (no IGETC) with a grade of "C" or better, complete additional coursework as required by the specific college at UCSD, and attend one of 15 specific community colleges (see Appendix "B"). The student must have a 2.8 GPA.

Santa Barbara

The SBCC/UCSB Transition Program available to students who attend Santa Barbara City, Allan Hancock, Ventura,

Moorpark, or Oxnard College. Students must meet UC minimum transfer admission requirements and complete an "admission agreement", which includes specific coursework and GPA requirements. Students are guaranteed admission into the College of Letters & Science, but not to specific majors.

Santa Cruz

The Guaranteed Admission Transfer Entry (GATE) requires a student to have a minimum of 30 UC transferable semester units, or less than 90 UC transferable semester units if combined with work from another university. However, to be eligible for GATE, a minimum GPA of 2.8 is required and the student must have completed at least 30 UC transferable semester units at a California community college, and be registered at one of the specific community colleges (see Appendix "B"). The program is available only for Fall admission.

Appealing

When a student does not get a favorable decision, appealing the decision is always an option even though there is no formal appeals process. Even though the UC campuses recommend appealing ". . .only when a student has new and compelling information," I never discourage an appeal. If a student can't discern the probable reason for their denial based on the information presented in this book, then a direct inquiry to the campus is in order. I personally know of situations where students were denied admission because of miscalculation of GPA and unit totals on the part of the admission reviewers. At the same time, students that want to appeal and are well below the recommended GPA, haven't completed significant coursework in the major or have not met minimum university admission requirements should not expect a favorable decision on their appeal. Over the years, the students that I have seen successfully appeal that have low

GPA's, usually had a bad start in college, took some time off, then came back and had two or three semesters of solid academic achievement

When crafting a letter of appeal, knowledge of the reason for denial can be helpful, but it is not critical. The letter should include a brief introduction, then the body should provide new information not already included in the essay or application. For example, previous poor performance should be addressed, specifically addressing factors that got in the way of the student's success and indicating what has changed. If a student has very specific academic reasons for wanting to attend the university, this should be made crystal clear in the appeal. Attaching letters of recommendation and progress reports from the classes that a student is currently enrolled in can be helpful. The recommendations should ideally come from teachers, and ideally from the specific discipline that a student wants to major in. I usually recommend no more than three letters, only because more letters would be overkill and probably annoy more than help. But remember, there is no formal process, and whatever a student chooses to do is their own business. Back in 1968, my sister was rejected from UCLA. She went to the Administration Building, and was able to see Chancellor Charles Young. She asked to be admitted. According to her, his response was, "Why should I admit you over all the others that were rejected?" She said, "Because I am here and they aren't." She was admitted.

Very Important Note and Conclusion

You have purchased the First Edition of *The Nannini Guide*. Although complete at publication, changes will occur in dealing with an intricate process that must meet eight different UC campuses' requirements. Consequently, as changes occur and new information arises, I will post this information free of charge on the web at:

www.transfertouc.com

This site will be useful in many aspects as we post the latest information that would interest or impact the transfer student or counselor.

I will do my professional best to stay on top of these changes, but I will need your help. When you get valid information related to transfer policies or information, please email me at either:

nannini_daniel@smc.edu or
nannini@transfertouc.com

After I validate the information, I will post it on the web. I will take all the updated information from the Web site and publish it in the second edition, and start the process over. Together, we can enhance a student's transition into the University of California.

Students: Work hard, ask questions, and get good counsel. You have more control of your destiny than you think. Make good decisions.

Counselors: One of the greatest pleasures of transfer counseling is mastering the detail so you can spend more time counseling. Listen for the unasked question, motivate, nurture and know that your work changes lives for the better.

Parents and significant others: Show your love by supporting and pushing those dear to you to reach their goals, even when either of you is tired, frustrated, or discouraged. Even if they don't say it, students need your help.

Glossary

❀ **AP (Advanced Placement):** An exam that students can take and receive college credit. Credit is determined by the college, school, or major at the UC campus that the student transfers to.

❀ **Appeals:** When a decision is rendered, on a petition or application, not in the favor of a student, the student provides additional documentation to the deciding party to receive a review for a favorable decision.

❀ **Articulation:** This is information about coursework from one college that indicates whether or not a course transfers to the University of California, and usually determines if that coursework is equivalent to either major requirements, general education requirements, or elective credit.

❀ **ASSIST:** A Web site that has articulation information between the community colleges and specific campuses of the University of California and some of the California State Universities. www.assist.org

❀ **Bachelors Degree (Baccalaureate):** The diploma awarded to an undergraduate that has completed all of the graduation requirements.

❀ **Campus:** The location of specific 10 UCs: Berkeley, Davis, Irvine, Los Angeles, Merced, Riverside, San Diego, San Francisco, Santa Barbara, Santa Cruz.

❀ **CAP (Cooperative Admissions Program):** A program for students eligible for UC freshman status but not admitted as freshmen. Allows the opportunity for lower division study at a community college with a guarantee of admission to Berkeley as a junior.

❖ **Catalog:** The dictionary, Yellow pages, and travel guide all rolled into one, which focuses on a specific campus. The information contained in the catalog covers policies and procedures for academic and non-academic affairs.

❖ **CCC:** California Community College

❖ **College:** A collection of departments and or majors connected together usually by an academic discipline or theme.

❖ **Department:** A specific unit that usually focuses on one specific field of academics, e.g. psychology or history.

❖ **EAP (Education Abroad Program):** A program of study at 120 colleges in 35 countries available in the junior year of undergraduate study ranging from one quarter to a full academic year. Transfer students may apply for EAP before enrolling at UC but only under certain conditions.

❖ **GATE (Guaranteed Admission for Transfer Entry):** A program that offers guaranteed admission to qualified junior level transfers to Santa Cruz from any of the 108 California community colleges that choose to participate.

❖ **General Education:** A broad smattering of courses to include a wide variety of subjects outside a specific major; also known as survey courses.

❖ **GPA (Grade Point Average):** A grading scale that ascribes point value to letter grades based on the number of units called grade points. A GPA is determined by the following formula: Total grade points for all coursework / total graded units attempted = GPA.

❖ **IB (International Baccalaureate):** An exam whereby a student can receive unit credit.

❖ **IGETC (Intersegmental General Education Transfer Curriculum):** A specific pattern of courses that completes General Education courses after transferring from a California community college for most UC Schools and Colleges.

❖ **Intercampus Transfer:** Some transfers within the UC campuses may be granted due to a student's personal circumstances and availability in the prospective major. An application must be submitted in a specified filing period. Some UC campuses do not accept any transfers who may have completed more than 120 quarter units.

❖ **Interdepartmental major:** A specific course of study usually grouped around a central theme that requires coursework from many different departments.

❖ **Lower Division:** A term used to describe courses that are usually taught the freshman or sophomore year of college and are general in content. California community colleges can only teach lower division courses.

❖ **Lower Division Major Preparation:** Lower division courses that are required as foundation information for upper division coursework. These courses are often comprised from a variety of departments. For example, engineering students are required to complete lower division courses in physics, chemistry, and math.

❖ **Major:** A specific course of study that is the focus of the undergraduate degree emphasizing one specific discipline.

❖ **Minor:** Additional coursework in a specific discipline other than the declared major, usually related to the major, but not always.

❀ **Mixed Record**: A student that has attended a university or baccalaureate granting college and a community college.

❀ **Petition**: The ability to ask for, in writing, a special exception to a specified rule or policy.

❀ **Quarter System**: The division of the academic year into four equal parts. All UCs, except Berkeley, are on a modified quarter system. In the UCs, three quarters constitute an academic year, with summer school considered an optional "quarter".

❀ **Re-entry Student**: An older, returning student. UC campuses provide programs and support services to assist all aspects of the a re-entry student's experience.

❀ **Repetition**: Repeating a course where a "D", "F", or "No Credit" (NC) was earned. A Withdraw ("W") is not considered a repetition.

❀ **SBCC/UCSB Transition Program**: A specific program is applied by only UC Santa Barbara for qualifying eligible transfer students from local community colleges.

❀ **School**: A school is a separate academic unit within a University.

❀ **Selection Criteria**: When a U. C. campus cannot admit all the eligible applicants, it applies standards that identify high academic achievers with other qualities that can contribute to the strength and diversity of the individual U. C. campus community.

❀ **Semester System**: The division of the academic year into two equal parts. Berkeley is the only UC campus on semester system.

❀ **Subject Credit**: When completing a course after the maximum units allowable for transfer, a student can earn credit for completion of the specific subject, yet receive no additional units or credits.

❊ **TAG (Transfer Admission Guarantee):** A program that assists students at participating community colleges in transferring to certain UC campuses.

❊ **TAP (Transfer Alliance Program):** A program that requires a rigorous honors/scholars program at a community college for transfer as a junior into certain UC campuses.

❊ **TCA (Transferable Course Agreement):** A document published by the University of California for every California Community College that determines the transferability of all courses from that community college.

❊ **UC:** University of California

❊ **Unit:** A specific measure of value ascribed to satisfactory completion a course of study. Sometimes referred to as credits or hours.

❊ **Unit Ceiling:** A maximum number of units allowed for completion of a Bachelors Degree.

❊ **Unit Credit:** Satisfactory completion of a course usually yields unit credit.

❊ **Upper Division:** A category of study at the undergraduate level that is more narrow in focus than lower division study. These courses are usually taught in the junior and senior years, and encompass most of the major.

❊ **WASC (Western Association of Schools and Colleges):** The accrediting agency for all UCs and California Community Colleges.

❊ **Well-Rounded Students:** Students who, in addition to their major, have completed a broad array of courses in different areas of study and have unique extracurricular experiences.

Appendix A:
Minimum UC Admission Criteria for Transfer Status Based on Requirements for Freshmen at the Time of High School Graduation

You will note that across the board, in all cases, a minimum GPA of a "C", (2.0) is required for all transferable coursework. The three qualifying avenues for transfer status based on UC's minimum eligibility requirements for freshmen at the time of their graduation from high school are:

1. "If you were eligible for admission to the University when you graduated from high school—meaning you satisfied the Subject, Scholarship, and Examination Requirements—you are eligible to transfer if you have a C (2.0) average in your transferable coursework.

2. If you met the Scholarship Requirement but did not satisfy the Subject Requirement, you must take transferable college courses in the missing subjects, earning a C or better in each required course, and have an overall C average in all transferable coursework to be eligible to transfer.

3. If you met the Scholarship Requirement but not the Examination Requirement, you must complete a minimum of 12 semester (18 quarter) units of transferable work and earn an overall C (2.0) average in all transferable college coursework completed.

Please consult "www.ucop.edu/pathways" for additional information.

(University of California 2001/2002 *Answers for Transfers*, Pg. 5)

Appendix B:
California Community Colleges (CCC) Participating in a Priority or Guaranteed Admissions Program in Agreement with Specific UC Campuses

Berkeley:

Cooperative Admissions Program (CAP) Letters and Science:

Alameda, Bakersfield, Cabrillo, Cañada, Chabot, Contra Costa, DeAnza, Diablo Valley, Foothill, Fresno City, Gavilan, Hartnell, Laney, Las Positas, Los Medanos, Marin, Mendocino, Merritt, Mission, Modesto Junior, Monterey Peninsula, Mount San Antonio, Napa Valley, Ohlone, Orange Coast, Sacramento City, Saddleback, San Diego City, San Diego Mesa, San Diego Miramar, City College of San Francisco, San Joaquin Delta, San Mateo, Santa Monica, Santa Rosa Junior, Skyline, Solano, Vista, and West Valley.

Cooperative Admissions Program (CAP) Environmental Design:

Chabot, Cosumnes River, Diablo Valley, Modesto Junior, Mount San Antonio, Orange Coast, Pasadena City, City College of San Francisco, San Mateo, and West Valley.

Cooperative Admissions Program (CAP) Engineering:

Chabot, Contra Costa, DeAnza, Diablo Valley, Evergreen Valley, Foothill, Fresno City, Laney, Marin, Merritt, Mission, Modesto, Ohlone, Sacramento City, City College of San

Francisco, San Joaquin Delta, San Mateo, Santa Rosa Junior, and Solano.

Cooperative Admissions Program (CAP) Natural Resources:

De Anza, Diablo Valley, Laney, Marin, City College of San Francisco, San Mateo and Santa Rosa.

Davis:

Transfer Opportunity Program (TOP):

American River, Cosumnes River, Cosumnes River/ Placerville, De Anza, Foothill, Laney, Los Medanos, Napa Valley, Sacramento City, San Jose City, Santa Rosa, Sierra, Solano Community, and West Valley.

Transfer Admission Agreements (TAAs):

Alameda, Bakersfield, Butte, Cabrillo, Chabot, Citrus, Columbia, Contra Costa, DeAnza, Diablo Valley, Foothill, Fresno, Gavilan, Hartnell, Kings River, Lake Tahoe, Las Positas, Lassen, Marin, Mendocino, Merritt, Mira Costa, Mission, Modesto, Monterey Peninsula, Ohlone, Porterville, College of the Redwoods, Saddleback, San Bernardino Valley, San Diego City, San Diego Mesa, San Diego Miramar, City College of San Francisco, San Joaquin Delta, San Jose City, San Mateo, Santa Barbara City, Santa Monica, College of the Sequoias, Shasta, College of the Siskiyous, Skyline, West Valley, Woodland Community, and Yuba.

Irvine:

Preliminary Admission in the Field:

Cerritos, Coastline Community, Cypress, East Los Angeles, El Camino, Fullerton, Glendale, Golden West, Irvine Valley, Long Beach City, Mount San Antonio, Orange Coast, Pasadena

City, Rio Hondo, Riverside City, Saddleback, Santa Ana, Santa Monica, and Santiago Canyon.

Community College Honors Transfer Program:

Allan Hancock, American River, Antelope Valley, Cerritos, Cerro Coso, Chaffey, College of the Canyons, Cypress, East Los Angeles, El Camino, Foothill, Fullerton, Glendale, Las Positas, Long Beach City, Los Angeles City, Los Angeles Harbor, Los Angeles Mission, Los Angeles Pierce, Los Angeles Southwest, Los Angeles Valley, Los Medanos, Mira Costa, Moorpark, Mt. San Antonio, Mt. San Jacinto, Orange Coast, Pasadena City, College of the Redwoods, Rio Hondo, Sacramento City, Saddleback, San Bernardino Valley, San Diego City, San Diego Mesa, San Diego Miramar, City College of San Francisco, Santa Ana, Santa Barbara City, Santa Monica, Santiago Canyon, West Los Angeles and West Valley.

Los Angeles:

Community College Transfer Program:

Antelope Valley, Cerritos, Chaffey, Citrus, College of the Canyons, Compton, Cypress, East Los Angeles, El Camino, Fullerton, Glendale, Golden West, Irvine Valley, Long Beach City, Los Angeles City, Los Angeles Harbor, Los Angeles Mission, Los Angeles Pierce, Los Angeles Southwest, Los Angeles Trade-Technical, Los Angeles Valley, Marymount Palos Verdes, Moorpark, Mount San Antonio, Orange Coast, Oxnard College, Pasadena City, Rio Hondo, Riverside City, Saddleback, San Bernardino Valley, Santa Ana, Santa Barbara City, Santa Monica, Santiago Canyon, Ventura, and West Los Angeles.

Transfer Alliance Program (TAP):

Antelope Valley, Cerritos, Cerro Coso, Chaffey, College of the Canyons, East Los Angeles, El Camino, Foothill, Fullerton, Glendale, Long Beach City, Los Angeles City, Los Angeles Harbor, Los Angeles Mission, Los Angeles Pierce, Los Angeles Southwest, Los Angeles Valley, Mt. San Antonio, Mt. San Jacinto, Orange Coast, Pasadena City, Rio Hondo, Saddleback, San Bernardino Valley, San Diego City, Santa Ana, Santa Monica, Santiago Canyon, West Los Angeles, and West Valley.

Riverside:

Transfer Admission Guarantee (TAG):

To be eligible, students must have attended only California community colleges.

San Diego:

Transfer Admission Guarantee (TAG):

Cuyamaca, DeAnza, Diablo Valley, Foothill, Grossmont, Imperial Valley, Mira Costa, Palomar, Pasadena City, Saddleback, San Diego City, San Diego Mesa, San Diego Miramar, Santa Barbara City, Santa Monica, Southwestern, and West Valley.

Santa Barbara:

SBCC/UCSB Transition Program:

Santa Barbara City College, Allan Hancock College, Moorpark College, Oxnard College, and Ventura College.

Santa Cruz:

Guaranteed Admission for Transfer Entry (GATE):

Alameda, Allan Hancock, American River, Antelope Valley, Bakersfield, Barstow, Butte, Cabrillo, Canada, Cerro Coso,

Chabot, Chaffey, Citrus, Columbia, Compton, Contra Costa, Copper Mountain, Cosumnes River, Cuesta, Cuyamaca, DeAnza, Diablo Valley, East Los Angeles, El Camino, Evergreen Valley, Feather River, Foothill, Fresno City, Fullerton, Gavilan, Glendale, Golden West, Grossmont, Hartnell, Imperial Valley, Lake Tahoe, Laney, Las Positas, Lassen, Los Angeles City, Los Angeles Mission, Los Angeles Pierce, Los Angeles Trade-Technical, Los Angeles Valley, Los Medanos, Marin, Mendocino, Merced, Merritt, Mira Costa, Mission, Modesto Junior, Monterey Peninsula, Moorpark, Mt. San Antonio, Mt. San Jacinto, Napa Valley, Ohlone, Orange Coast, Oxnard, Palomar, Pasadena City, Porterville, College of the Redwoods, Reedley, Riverside, Sacramento City, Saddleback, San Diego Mesa, San Diego Miramar, City College of San Francisco, San Joaquin Delta, San Jose City, San Mateo, Santa Ana, Santa Barbara City, Santa Monica, Santa Rosa Junior, Santiago Canyon, College of the Sequoias, Shasta, Sierra, College of the Siskiyous, Skyline, Solano, Southwestern, Ventura, West Hills, West Los Angeles, West Valley, and Yuba.

Please consult the publication *Answers for Transfer* located on the web site:www.ucop.edu/pathways for additional information.